rhubarb

by

Tom Jenks

published by Beir Bua Press

www.BeirBuaPress.com

Dedication -

Thanks to the editors of the following publications, in which some of these pieces first appeared: The Abandoned Playground, Confingo, Litter, The Manchester Review, Mercurius, Okay Donkey, Periodicities, Perverse, Poetry Review, Queen Mob's Teahouse, Spelk.

ISBN: 978-1-914972-23-2

Beir Bua Press, Co. Tipperary, Ireland.

Typesetting / Layout, Cover Design: Michelle Moloney King. Cover image: Michelle Moloney King

Ordering Information: For details, see www.BeirBuaPress.com

Published by Beir Bua Press. Printed in the UK

Our printer is certified as a B Corporation to measure our impact on the environment and help drive us to be even more conscious of our footprint.

A short essay on rhubarb

I once ate six helpings of school dinner rhubarb. They needed to get rid of it and no-one wanted it except me. I kept coming back, even after the custard was gone, even when the ladle was going so deep into the steel vat that the rhubarb had a sharp, jangling taste, like licking a battery. It seemed that I liked rhubarb more than other people liked rhubarb, an important lesson. It would have been legendary, if anyone had noticed.

I still like rhubarb. I seem to mention it a lot in my work. I wrote a story called 'rhubarb', which is in this collection, also called 'rhubarb'. I like the word 'rhubarb' too. I like its wayward 'h', pushing up through the other letters like rhubarb pushes up through cracks in a patio, finding its way in like rhubarb finds its way into suburban gardens from waste ground and sidings. If you were so inclined, you could see this as saying something about the way I write, my interest in the unplanned and the persistent, in what is really there rather than what is meant to be there, in the provisional, the contingent, in what happens in sheds.

Say 'rhubarb' twice and you have 'rhubarb rhubarb', which is used to indicate background noise, general hubbub. Again, if you were so inclined, you could see this as saying something about the way I write, my interest in the background rather than the foreground, in unofficial chit-chat rather than proper conversations. After all, who's interested in proper conversations?

This pamphlet collects a number of pieces written over a number of years. Thanks to all who previously published, supported and otherwise indulged me. I almost called this book 'flamingos' but I couldn't stand on one leg for long enough.

eyebrows

When I return from my walk across the fields,
my mother trims my eyebrows with the kitchen scissors.

They grow two centimetres every day.
The air is fertile out here in the country.

As she snips, she talks about my father
and the rate at which his eyebrows grew:

five centimetres some days, others not at all.
He was that sort of a man, inconsistent in his habits.

He never kissed me on the mouth she says
only on the elbow or just below the kneecap.

I look at her kneecaps. They are strong and sturdy.
My mother has the legs of a Russian gymnast.

They do not falter as she carries me upstairs
and lays me down on the wrong side of the bed.

While I sleep, she gazes across the fields,
scissors at the ready, knees and elbows bared.

The curate passes on his bicycle,
three times, slowly, his eyebrows on fire.

Monsieur Dupont

What do you think about this cheese? It is sturdy, it is good for sauces.
It is summer and I wear two shirts. I read about it in the inflight magazine.
I like holes better with something in them, like marmalade or a type of gravel.
I like to like things before others like them, then I like to stop liking them:
soya milk in Earl Grey (you've heard of it) a tiny green flash in the toaster slot,
other things like rain in a bucket, or the blue glass ashtray my parents had.

When we're bored of skating, we set off the extinguishers.
We are bored of fire, fire is so over, no-one likes fire anymore.
I am in poor health, tenuous, pursued by magicians.
They put reticulated pythons in my dreams and thwart me at the serving hatch.
If you see me down the tavern, I'm training to be a highwayman.
I'm a highwayman, my name it is Overnight Oats.

not so fast, Fyodor

The tragically overlooked nineteenth century Russian novelist
places a One Cup drawstring teabag in a dishwasher-safe cup
and fills the cup with hot water
from the wall-mounted Zip HydroBoil instant hot water boiler.

The tragically overlooked nineteenth century Russian novelist
is melancholy, as always, ruminatively eating a muesli bar,
gazing out over the rooftops of the supermarket
and the smaller surrounding shops.

One shop sells paperbacks, but nothing worth having.
Another sells miniature jars of artisan jam.

The tragically overlooked nineteenth century Russian novelist's
behaviour in meetings has been remarked upon, unfavourably.
He has been accused of sighing, fidgeting,
putting his head in his hands and being generally distracted.

He has been accused of extracting a pale blue egg
from within his knotted, straw-coloured beard
and cracking it into his mouth
during the virtual wellness huddle,
an accusation that is largely unsubstantiated.

The really tragic thing is that no-one is aware that
the tragically overlooked nineteenth century Russian novelist
is a tragically overlooked nineteenth century Russian novelist.

This fact, it seems, has been inadequately documented.

when it gets dark, I fetch my special spoon

I drank nothing but celery juice for seven days.
I ran around the internet and wore antlers wired to the moon.
I was steward of the roots that twist in the ground,
sundry silver pools.

Is it true that UHT milk cures everything
if you rub it on a sponge
and then rub the sponge on a bit of yourself.
This is not a joke, this is grave.

Listen doc, I am coming down with it.

I have a fat, domed belly full of pasta.
I eat because of emotional conflict,
which I represent unflinchingly.
I get drunk with the wood elves out in the National Park.
We bang our thumbs with hammers
and our thumbs they do throb.

Can you do anything about these, they are hanging down.
Can you give me something to tie them up, like twine
or the string they use for hams.

When we couldn't get conkers, we used water chestnuts
which were a waste product then, like goose fat or memories.

hedge

We have planted a hedge at the edge of the fields. It grows a little each day, like our ardour. At night we stand either side of it and picture it seven feet tall, with a ditch.

bushes

There is no consolation in cauliflower cheese
or visiting the forest to find it empty.
We spent the summer at the chateau near the ice rink,
opening and closing the tumble drier,
playing Subbuteo in the long room where you wrote
The Top 9 Rules That Successful People Live By.

Little wasps with shells of earthenware.
You break open the shell of earthenware,
and there is another shell of earthenware.
All the different pasta, the absurdity of it.

We burnt our mouths on pumpkin gnocchi
and cried for six weeks straight on the ramparts.
This is a feast day, circled on the planner,
when we can eat as much frozen spinach as we please,
when a window opens to his lordship's larder
and there we may touch the caramels, for miracles.

Some things are pointless, like meringues are pointless,
or golf balls, or history, or telling a joke to dolphins
that does not specifically reference dolphins is pointless.

People change, but a lemon remains a lemon.

That is an interesting philosophical position, said the gnome,
absent-mindedly folding a crepe suzette.
Let's go outside and wave at the space station.

Most days, I think I am finished, said the gnome,
distractedly toying with a balloon whisk.
Sometimes I get a really good idea,
but my pen is on the other side of the kingdom.

We are inert, the gnome and I,
like the noble gases and multigrain boulders.
We have slept too long in the yellow moonlight,
desolate in a world of fondant.
We are stone cold, mostly, or else burnt out.
Often, we get lost in the bushes.

eggs

We drank the milk of gentle goats
and threw the eggs into the river.
We made a bonfire of tiny chairs.
We picked wild rocket and put it on pizza.
We wrote a song about the eggs
and how we threw them into the river.
We sang our song about the eggs.
We grew wild thyme and put it on pasta.
How happy we are without the eggs
now that they are in the river,
there amongst the white and brown stones,
no-one knowing one from the other.

song from the forest

What can I do with him, he is so randy,
hairy hands in the mayonnaise.
Long evening in the bungalow
discussing at length the artificial ski slope,
baleful light on fruiting bushes
and frightful permutations of celery.

We pass a winter with the wolves,
so cruel and yet emotionally literate,
rising in spring to fulfil our destiny
and live amongst the plankton farmers,
there to compose our power ballads
and stir their souls with special pumps.

I work from notes these days, my love,
for I am not the man that once I was,
when you watched me stride through the reference section
with Michael Bolton, my steadfast falcon.

Oh cold pressed tongue how sweet you sing of larks and other flying things,
buttered soft in Birkenhead, briskly frisked in Rivendell.

Startled again in the walk-in pantry,
I scorched my appendage in the sandwich toaster
and cried out, knowing myself forsaken
by all except the Kenwood Chef,

in these, the most indifferent of times,
zoned out once more in the strategy meeting,
traduced by rooks at the business park.

peaches

The remaining peaches made a sorbet so crisp and cold the district nurse lost control of her moped, momentarily.

Humboldt

The Humboldt squid lives predominately upstairs,
coming down for meals, parcel deliveries
or to demonstrate his particular skills.

'Look', says the Humboldt squid;
'I am cracking this troublesome coconut with my beak'.
'Look', says the Humboldt squid.
'With this tentacle, I am stirring porridge.
With this tentacle, I am poaching an egg
using the whirlpool method.
With this tentacle, I am learning ju-jitsu online.
With this tentacle, I am casting runes.
With this tentacle, I am writing a screenplay
in which a large squid designed to live
in the deep waters of the Humboldt current,
which flows northwest from Tierra del Fuego
to the northern coast of Peru
is instead living in a three-bedroom suburban semi-detached
which has a problem with fruit flies in summer
and a Wi-Fi connection that is affected by the weather'.

We are all of us balanced on this seesaw, I say.
We dip our hands into the jar, but the jar is made of opaque glass
and there is no way to know exactly what is in the jar.

'I worry', says the Humboldt squid
'that you will die and I won't feel anything,
also how, in that eventuality,
I will push down the plunger of the cafetiere
without spilling coffee over the work surface'.

Meals are mainly prawns and spaghetti
eaten with the lights off and the TV on.
There is an ornate butter knife on the table between us,
its handle encrusted with polished shells.

One of us will reach for it.

pops

'Why don't we get a camper van', said Pops,
'and take our wisdom to the mountain folk?'
That's a great idea Pops, but we're not going to do it.
Camper vans don't grow on trees
and wisdom turns to folly north of the snowline.

We decant the linctus into silver vials
and hide them down the cul-de-sac.
Your trouble is you know nothing of love,
playing slide trombone in your loft conversion.

All true poets are sad on the inside,
like giant pandas or Olympic athletes.
The mountain folk are something else.

They shear their llamas and sing ballads about whales.
They shoot an arrow into the forest
and wherever it lands they build a monument.
This one shows where the king lost his waffles.

complicated

I woke up in the llama enclosure.
As always, they were kind,
drying me with their fleeces,
gently exfoliating my forehead with their tongues.
'Maybe I should move in permanently', I say,
but they don't reply,
knowing this to be complicated, administratively.

ducks

The druids are back,

splitting their shopping into separate transactions,
explaining everything they're doing while they're doing it.

'Observe, Margaret', says the one in the snood
'how I trim the ancient holly with scissors,
 which both improves its silhouette and encourages fruition.'

These are curious times.
The ducks have left town.
Stars overlap above the business park,
where latterly there have been unexplained bin fires.

lute

The sage says we should reject books
and learn from nature.

'Consider, he says, the salad.
'Consider the carrots, so orange.
 Consider the lettuce, so green.
 Consider the tomatoes, so red.
 Consider the pine nuts, so rich in protein.'

We say we don't hold with pine nuts.
We get protein from rind
and drinking the blood of our enemies.

'Things are different in the southern kingdoms', the sage says.
'They have milk that isn't milk.
 They sculpt their hair with putty.'

The Great Hall falls silent.
Pickles, the bard, lays down his lute.

ox

An emissary brings news from the north,
a rival kingdom providing photocopying at 3p a sheet
and free extended warrantees on white goods.

'How are the numbers', asks the king,
knowing they are bad,
having seen the plummeting lines,
the charts shaded red.

'Maybe', he suggests, 'we should offer gifts:
 monogrammed USB sticks,
 or child-safe glow products.'

The courtiers sigh.
He is half the man his ancestors were.
His father could roll a cigarette on horseback.
His grandfather overcame an ox.

Walt Disney is sending us letters

The postman brings them down the cinder path, across the rustic bridge.

Walt Disney's letters are postmarked with the silhouette of a castle.
Walt Disney's letters are in envelopes made from thick, creamy paper,
like you might buy in a department store in a foreign city.
But Walt Disney's letters are written on thin blue paper,
cheap and poor quality.
Sometimes, the paper is damp
and the ink on Walt Disney's letters is blurred.
This is a problem,
for it is important that Walt Disney's letters are legible.

We are deep in the forest.
We listen to the wind in the trees.
There are birds and a river.
Rain falls amidst plants and trees.

'It is beautiful here', says the knight.
'It is boring here', says the knight.

We play our wooden flutes and study our reflections.
We make rudimentary weapons from fallen wood.
'We should not be complacent', says the knight.
'We may be attacked at any time.
 Something may issue from the swamp,
 a Komodo dragon or a giant talking dog.'
Walt Disney's charms will not help us, as they are powered by starlight
and there are no stars this deep within the trees.

The knight's armour is embossed with an eagle and the Coca-Cola logo.
The knight feigns nonchalance,
but awaits Walt Disney's letters with eagerness
lingering by the rustic bridge to intercept the postman.

When one of Walt Disney's letters arrives, the utensils vibrate.
The saucepans rattle. The spoons turn their blank faces towards
the window, where rain is falling.

Rain on the giant red cedar, the cathedral fig.
Rain on the banana trees, the kapok trees, the strangler fig.
New hair grows on our shoulders.
There is nothing to feel guilty about.

Walt Disney signs the letters with a self-inking stamp.
Walt Disney must press down repeatedly to produce a signature.

Walt Disney says that dreams come true if we pursue them.
Walt Disney says that we must keep our aim
constantly focused on the future.
Walt Disney wanders the forest, amongst fauns and princesses.
Walt Disney says that gardens are an abomination,
 that nature should be wild.

'Not every rabbit is a lucky rabbit', mutters the knight,
staring darkly into a pool.

The sounds of thunder and rain in the foggy forest
create calming white noise.
Birds perch on the watchtower, high on a pinnacle.
We look at the birds through binoculars.
The birds appear seven times closer.

Walt Disney wears a cape and a pair of mouse ears.
Walt Disney appears as a duck or a hallucinogenic mushroom.
Moonlight filters onto cobblestones.

White smoke billows from the cottage chimney.
Everything is ordered by enchantments.
Elastic bands coalesce into balls.
Equations appear on the walls and are resolved,
amongst watercolours of dogs, roads, mountains and food.

There are three hours of gentle rain.
It is dark, and the rain is just visible.

Walt Disney is not in the forest tonight.
Walt Disney is in his cellar, converted into a home gym.

Walt Disney uses the assisted pull-up machine.
Walt Disney wants to get ripped for the princesses.
Walt Disney counts the seconds on his classic quartz analogue watch.
Walt Disney follows The Ultimate Arms Workout Plan.

We sit beside a crackling fire.
We drink cherry brandy, sweet vermouth and lychee juice.
We are burning birch wood, which burns cleanly.
The cherry blossom is in full bloom.
Birdsong fills the air.

Walt Disney is in a high room
writing letters to the children of the world,
trimming his moustache with silver scissors,
sweetening coffee with saccharine.
Which way does Walt Disney stir his coffee?
It is impossible to say.

White noise streams on TVs on different floors.
Wind distresses the ornate fluting of the abandoned watchtower.
It makes for calm and restful sleep.

The knight sleeps where he falls, on a heap of fire-retardant cushions
piled serendipitously near the ventilation shaft.
In his dreams, he sings of gold.

Walt Disney is alone in his high room, painting chaffinches.
The knight talks in his sleep.

The light from Walt Disney's high room
may just be the light of the moon.
The knight says that when he dies,

he wants his head to be cryogenically frozen
so that he can be revived by future scientific advances.

But what, I ask the knight, will he do when he is revived?

Walt Disney's pen is poised over a sheet of yellow paper,
his pen filled with aquamarine ink.

peaches

No good can come from all this information. We lock the telephone in the chest freezer, snip the wires with toenail scissors, remove the batteries from the squirrels. Friends ask our opinion. They read realist novelists and are serious. We say there are no opinions, just like there are no ostriches. We write poems in the early mornings, before the postman brings the butter. We pour ourselves a glass of peaches and know there is nothing to be done.

the baby

(i)

You should value the time before the baby. You should stay in bed and eat luxury ice cream and chilled exotic fruit because you can't do that when the baby is here. You should pursue leisure interests because the baby will put a stop to those. You should visit galleries and encounter meaningful works of art, taking notes to share with the baby at a later date. You should read the books and dossiers about the baby that have been provided. You should pay particular attention to the highlighted passages as they are of particular relevance to the baby. You should make sure you are prepared for when the baby arrives.

(ii)

You should be aware that the baby may arrive at an importune time, such as during a meal or approaching the tense conclusion of a board game. You should make sure the baby feels welcome. You should offer the baby a handshake and make eye contact with the baby and say you are very glad the baby is here. You should take the baby to the room you have prepared. You should show the baby the geopolitical globe with the major powers delineated. You should show the baby the shelf of encyclopaedias with facts and diagrams of climate change. You should show the baby the working model of the solar system.

(iii)

You should explain to the baby that the working model of the solar system isn't to scale because that would place Pluto in an adjoining property. You should explain to the baby that the working model of the solar system includes Pluto as it is somewhat antiquated. You should monitor the baby closely. You should check the baby's progress against agreed milestones. You should subject the baby to light, sound and other stimuli. You should read the recommended texts to the baby, with simple, compelling narratives and underlying messages. You should not expose the baby to authorial unreliability. You should take the baby out. You should bring the baby home again.

(iv)

You should ensure the baby is inside normal ranges and make adjustments if the baby is outside normal ranges. You should plot progress on a chart with the baby being the x axis. You should give the baby pulverised tubers. You should not give the baby bad fat. You should give the baby digestible rice. You should not give the baby lightly cooked eggs. You should give the baby unsweetened yogurt. You should not give the baby some cheeses. You should familiarise yourself with when the baby likes to sleep and attend to circadian rhythms. You should know about the moon and how the moon affects the baby by secret magnets.

(v)

You should look up into the sky with the baby in the small hours and tell the baby the names of the things that are in the sky. You should tell the baby the various names of birds. You should encourage birds to perch to show the baby and say to the baby to look at the birds there in the moonlit kitchen. You should play the baby forest sounds. You should pass over in silence the things that dwell in the forest as these may disquiet the baby. You should not mention the mysterious horned figure who dwells amongst the knotted brambles beyond the rabbit proof fence to the baby.

(vi)

You should encourage the baby to sit. You should encourage the baby to stand. You should encourage the baby to crawl by providing meaningful incentives. You should encourage the baby to walk by stressing the core message of self-reliance. You should encourage the baby to remain within the carpeted and lawned areas. You should remind the baby of its fontanelle. You should warn the baby that the flowers are poisonous and can cause hypotension and hypertension. You should develop an effective communication style to communicate with the baby, utilising key words and phrases. You should remark to the baby that communication is only seven percent verbal and is ninety-three percent non-verbal.

(vii)

You should show the baby the smoke signals over the pass indicating that something is awry. You should show the baby the telegrams that arrive erratically, brought over rough country by horse. You should ensure the baby is apprised of events. You should demonstrate the movements of submarines beneath the icecap with objects so that the baby can follow them. You should ensure that the baby has habits which will give the baby a solid foundation and a lifetime of health. You should teach the baby that nature does not hurry, yet everything is accomplished. You should teach the baby that the more water there is, the higher the boat rises.

(viii)

You should not be alarmed when the baby no longer needs you. You should not take offence when the baby turns away when you are talking and gazes into the distance towards the mountains or a neighbouring province. You should not be nonplussed when the baby begins to communicate with other babies by passing coded messages in crayon or along the pipes. You should make time for yourself as well as for the baby. You should eat boneless duck and a luxury platter while the baby is happily occupied with a task or its own thoughts. You should watch with pride as the baby erects structures from age appropriate building materials.

(ix)

You should not be disappointed when the baby decides to raze these structures. You should hold regular meetings in which the baby is invited to play a meaningful role in shaping the future direction of the organisation. You should tell the baby that great things never come from comfort zones. You should tell the baby that the key to success is to focus on goals not obstacles. You should give the baby probiotic powders. You should keep the baby away from predatory animals. You should teach the baby unarmed combat. You should enjoy the baby. You should remind yourself and the baby that this is the best time of your life.

friends

Most days, I don't bother getting dressed,
just fasten my tunic with paperclips.
I type a message in the chat box. I say:
'I note you have ceased putting gunk on your forelock.'
I dream I am the rhino, prized for my horn.
The shelf is falling down and the eggs roll off it.
I am much funnier than Mike,
and Mike is 'England's most amusing heron'.
Please forward this to seventeen friends, signed
Lots of love, Mr and Mrs Emily Dickinson.

Michael

Michael explains the working model
in the Social Sciences Seminar Room.
'The bubbly rash has reappeared', says Michael;
'and I can't help finding that significant.'
The island is encircled by birds
and things that grew too big to keep.
We hide the speedboat in the bulrushes
but still the Swedish collectors uncover it.
Michael draws a map in the sand
and colour codes the lorry terminus.
Michael writes a poem in the sand
and puts a link to it in his bio.

Dimples

Dimples eats from the trough of the world.
He tampers with the thermostat so we think we have malaria.
He boils up cabbage and calls it a sauna.
He squirts the toothpaste deliberately on his lips.
He sours the milk with his hairdryer.
He pulls up a chair and stands on it
to treat us to The Wisdom of Dimples, e.g.:
(i)   *never judge a book by its bookmark*
(ii) *never keep a box inside the box you're keeping it in*
(iii) *if you lie down with biscuits, you're going to get crumbs*

We gather in the garden at dusk,
while Dimples works on his novel.
'I'm fed up with Dimples', says Dimples' brother,
whose name is also Dimples.
'I too am fed up with Dimples', says Dimples' sister,
whose name is also Dimples,
or the female equivalent of Dimples.

'I am similarly fed up with Dimples', I say;
'I abhor Dimples like the cartoon cat abhors the cartoon dog,
like the small fish abhors the slightly larger fish,
like the lollipop abhors the stick what sticks it.'
Dimples' brother and Dimples' sister pause,
their soya lattes frozen midway to their lips.
'That is exactly something Dimples would say', they say.

Where is Dimples anyway?
His room is empty, his towel neatly folded on his bed.
The moon shines on it and the desk he sits at.

zoom

They put on a toaster on Mars.
It was all going great, until they realised
they'd forgotten to send up any bread.
'Who was on bread?' demanded the mission controller,
furiously tugging at his epaulettes.
No-one answered.
All they could do was watch the little handle go down
and then pop up again.
Also, the camera was really blurred.
You could only just make out the words *Morphy Richards*
on 200% zoom.

firewood

I visited Fat Larry in his cave where he has lived since his death in 1987, five years after the release of his worldwide hit 'Zoom'.

The cave was sparsely furnished with a black ash table and atmospheric lighting. I asked what he had been doing.

'Taekwondo', said Fat Larry, 'and closeup magic.'

I asked what he ate.

'Pop Tarts', he said, 'preferably frosted.'

Sometimes, he licked the rock for minerals.

'Look', said Fat Larry; 'these carvings describe my worldwide hit 'Zoom'. The undulating line is my distinctive synthesiser sound.'

I asked what configuration of stalactites and stalagmites was required. Fat Larry said it was more important that they were in equal proportions.

Fat Larry said he hoped to return to earth. He was writing a magical realist novel about a 1980s pop star who lived in a cave and mastered martial arts and sorcery.

It could become a film starring Michael Douglas.

Failing that, he would become a highwayman.

I said there was little call for them these days. He should become something more contemporary, like a beekeeper, a chocolatier or a life coach.

Vibrations indicated darkness had descended.

'The moon and stars came out to play', said Fat Larry as we chopped up the black ash table for firewood.

raspberries

You notice you've started to grunt when rising from the sofa, like your grandfather did before you, ambling to the mouth of the cave to confidently predict a storm, or to tend the raspberries, silver with frost.

profiteroles

We got a python and the python was small,
but now the python has grown considerably larger
and no longer fits inside its travel sleeve,
which cost £18.99, plus postage.

It is a tragedy, like my poem
'The Ghost who Neglected Vitamins'
or 'Centrefold' by the J Geils band.

None of the old spells work
and there are ants in the salad cream.

You should always start by clearly defining the problem
and remember that you don't need to tell everybody everything.

There was a fire in the product development kitchen,
and all the experimental cheese is ruined,
moreover there is fondue on the awning.

There are hazelnuts and blueberry foam.
There is marmalade and we spread it on each other.

A passing heron visits the aquarium
and invalidates the record attempt.
It is nearly harvest and there is no quiche,
just eggs and cheese kept separately.

Perhaps there is no product development kitchen,
just a series of garages, artfully fitted with steam and alcoves.
No-one cares about eggs and cheese,
or things made from eggs and cheese.

Ball pythons are so named
because they roll into a ball when threatened.
Young ball pythons grow about a foot a year for three years.
They can live for 20-30 years with proper care.
You should never feed them profiteroles,
even if they ask insistently,
in that voice so smooth, like butterscotch or honey.

scissors

Syrup on soya, the square holes in waffles,
cheesy dumplings, ancient grain rolls,
I don't know what to make of any of it.
All the elements for a good life are in place,
yet a good life is not being lived.
We should rethink the solar system
or buy each other shoulder bags.
I saw a dog that was entirely see through.
I've got a ride on mower
but I still use scissors.

opportunities

The horse was revealed to be entirely two-dimensional. This presented challenges, but also opportunities.

saccharine

The museum has paintings of mountains, heroic scenes and food. There are working models of turbines, a famous vase you can look inside and a stuffed lion with green glass eyes. If approached with humility and addressed by its lion name, the lion will tell the future: this weekend's numbers, the fate of the harvest, the date of the next shipwreck. If addressed by the name given to it by humans, the lion will feign incomprehension, gazing stonily through the long windows and across the fields sloping down to the sea. None of us knows the lion's lion name. We try random combinations of letters in the fine dust on the display cases. We sit in the cafeteria playing spot the ball, trapped in the present, pouring long-life milk into our instant coffee, sweetening it with saccharine.

gnomes

The gnomes congregate in the conservatory to smoke their pipes and listen to Syd Barrett. I try to make conversation, asking about their hats and fishing, but they ignore me, guzzling Black Forest gateau, which they buy at the freezer centre in the precinct, where they've negotiated credit.

sisters

I tied the dog to a tree outside the snooker hall. When I returned, the tree had been replaced with an exact replica of the tree and the dog replaced with a replica of the dog, also exact apart from the name engraved on the little bone-shaped tag. But it was a brisk morning, the DJs playing martial music and the songs of the Minogue sisters and no time to quibble over details.

bear

The bear costume hangs on the garage door.
It rarely has an outing these days.
It's all foxes and rabbits
in the smart places now,
and squirrels with waistcoats and lavish tails.
The bear costume reproaches me
when I'm on the exercise bike
its plastic eyes profound and forlorn.
My heart flutters
like a chaffinch in a shoe box
or the fluttering heart of a bear who,
after using his astounding strength
to gain access to a family car at a beauty spot,
struggles to open the glove compartment
and accidentally turns on the radio.

bears

The bears grow bolder, crossing the main road, hanging around the petrol station. Yesterday, we watched one cram his giant paw into a disposable plastic glove whilst the others looked on. When our stipend arrives, we will buy yellow cream, for the storks, and apples, for the bears. Cooking apples are best, good and heavy, thudding on the forest floor.

rhubarb

Stanley is up early cutting the rhubarb. He uses the heavy knife with the weathered handle. He curses when a stalk is stubborn, or the knife cuts his thumb instead of the rhubarb. He invokes our saviour and all the saints. He puts the rhubarb in the big pan with the lost lid.

Some is for pies and crumbles. Some is for rhubarb jelly, with ginger for flavour and lemon juice for the necessary pectin. The rest is for rhubarb gin. Stanley curses the rhubarb but loves rhubarb gin. I would say this was ironic, but irony is a difficult concept.

What is edible is established by trial and error. Stanley himself established the rhubarb as edible. The orange flowers beneath the elms were established as inedible by one of the cats. Stanley ground up some petals and mixed them with mackerel. The cat went under the table and stayed there for a long time. It was thinking about its past. Stanley says that cats have a capacity for introspection that dogs lack. It's why Stanley prefers cats to dogs.

Stanley visits friends over the fields. Windows glow through dark trees. He takes rhubarb gin and orange flowers. He picks a careful path, skirting insuperable obstacles. He passes a convivial evening. The orange flowers go in a white jug. There is cake and brittle. Conversation concerns local issues, such as the restoration fund, the problem of fouling and how to prevent crown rot, which afflicts rhubarb when soil becomes waterlogged. Stanley says that local issues are the only important issues.

Stanley's trip home takes longer. He proceeds with less caution. He blunders into thickets. I go out with the heavy knife to free him. He will curse and petition the fiends and fallen angels of Hell. If the windows are open, you will hear laughter and music. If the windows are closed, there will just be my breathing, Stanley's breathing and the swish of the heavy knife.

Stanley may need reassurance. We will lay out the documents and consult them systematically. One of the cats will come close, sniff Stanley's breath and detect the unmistakable rhubarb. If

Stanley needs a remedy, there is neutralising cordial, made with rhubarb tincture, cinnamon tincture, hydrastis tincture and spirit of peppermint, or colon tonic, made with Oregon grape, cayenne, lobelia and rhubarb root.

Rhubarb is used medicinally in countless cultures. The Chinese call rhubarb 'the great yellow'. Rhubarb is pink, mixed with green. No matter how much Stanley cuts it, the rhubarb grows back. It is perennial with abiding roots. It is entrenched under the hard standing. It is a rugged species. Stanley says that the rhubarb will outlast us, like the stars. People have puzzled over them for centuries. No-one's come up with anything concrete.

reply all (a sonnet)

I think I have been sent this in error!
I think I have been sent this in error as well!
Think I have too!
Me too!
I have too.
I think you may have sent this in error.
Don't think this is for me.

Stop replying please.
Please stop replying to the original email.
Please don't reply all, I have a million emails.
Please can we stop, my inbox is going crazy.

Please stop sending reply all!!!!!!!!!!
PLEASE DO NOT REPLY TO THIS EMAIL.

Bio.:

Tom Jenks writes poetry and short prose and runs the avant-objects imprint zimZalla. More at https://www.zshboo.org

Blurbs.:

"Traversing the business parks of the world with mythical creatures riding shotgun, rhubarb offers up a must-have companion to a skewed reality, with plenty of sage advice and witty repartee perfect for parties in the new normal; tightly written user manuals for our own "big pan with the lost lid".

- **Sarah-Clare Conlon; Manchester-based writer and editor; pamphlets 2022 with Contraband and Broken Sleep.**

"Tom Jenks' poetry is as mysterious as it is funny, like some playful cousin of the citizenship test, it stares down contemporary Britishness and nails the horror."

- **Sophie Herxheimer is an artist and poet who lives in South London.**

"Squid learn ju-jitsu online, overlooked Russian novelists fail to avoid virtual wellness huddles; the genius of Tom Jenks can be found in his surreal intricacies, his throwaway profundities, his delicious deadpan and in that feeling he leaves you with, not sure whether to laugh or cry."

- **Vik Shirley, poet, writer & editor of *Mercurius* Surreal-Absurd.**

Printed in Great Britain
by Amazon